THAI PENAL CODE

OFFENCE AGAINST LIFE AND BODY, OFFENCE AGAINST LIBERTY AND REPUTATION, OFFENCE AGAINST PROPERTY

SP

© Copyright 2021 by SP - All rights reserved.

The following Book is reproduced below with the goal of providing information that is as accurate and reliable as possible. Regardless, purchasing this Book can be seen as consent to the fact that both the publisher and the author of this book are in no way experts on the topics discussed within and that any recommendations or suggestions that are made herein are for entertainment purposes only. Professionals should be consulted as needed prior to undertaking any of the action endorsed herein.

This declaration is deemed fair and valid by both the American Bar Association and the Committee of Publishers Association and is legally binding throughout the United States.

Furthermore, the transmission, duplication, or reproduction of any of the following work including specific information will be considered an illegal act irrespective of if it is done electronically or in print. This extends to creating a secondary or tertiary copy of the work or a recorded copy and is only allowed with the express written consent from the Publisher. All additional right reserved.

The information in the following pages is broadly considered a truthful and accurate account of facts and as such, any inattention, use, or misuse of the information in question by the reader will render any resulting actions solely under their purview. There are no scenarios in which the publisher or the original author of this work can be in any fashion deemed liable for any hardship or damages that may befall them after undertaking information described herein.

Additionally, the information in the following pages is intended only for informational purposes and should thus be thought of as universal. As befitting its nature, it is presented without assurance regarding its prolonged validity or interim quality. Trademarks that are mentioned are done without written consent and can in no way be considered an endorsement from the trademark holder.

Table of contents

CHAPTER 1 6

CHAPTER 2 16

CHAPTER 3 19

CHAPTER 4 22

CHAPTER 5 24
    OFFENCE OF ABANDONMENT OF CHILDREN, SICK PERSONS OR AGED PERSONS 24

CHAPTER 6 26
    OFFENCE AGAINST LIBERTY 26

CHAPTER 7 35

CHAPTER 8 37

CHAPTER 10 40
    OFFENCE OF THEFT AND SNATCHING 40

CHAPTER 11 46

CHAPTER 12 53
    OFFENCE OF CHEATING AND FRAUD 53

CHAPTER 13 57

CHAPTER 14 59

CHAPTER 15 62

CHAPTER 16 64

CHAPTER 17 67

CHAPTER 18 70

PETTY OFFENCES 70

CHAPTER 1

OFFENCE RELATING TO SEXUALITY

Section 276 Whoever has sexual intercourse with a woman, who is not wife, against her will, by threatening by any means whatever, by doing any act of violence, by taking advantage of the woman being in the condition of inability to resist, or by causing the woman to mistake him for the other person, shall be punished with imprisonment of four to twenty years and fined of eight thousand to forty thousand Baht.

If the offence as mentioned in the first paragraph is committed by carrying or using any gun or explosive, or participation of persons in the nature of destroying the woman, the offender shall be punished with imprisonment of fifteen to twenty years and fined of thirty thousand to forty thousand Baht, or imprisonment for life.

Section 277 Whoever, has sexual intercourse with a girl not yet over fifteen years of age and not being his own wife, whether such girl shall consent or not, shall be punished with imprisonment of four to twenty years and fined of eight thousand to forty thousand Baht. If the commission of the offence according to the first paragraph is committed against a girl not yet over thirteen years of age, the offender shall be punished with imprisonment of seven to twenty years and fined of fourteen thousand to forty thousand Baht, or imprisonment for life.

If the commission of the offence according to the first or second paragraph is committed by participation of persons in the nature for destroying a girl and such girl is not consent, or by carrying the gun or explosive, or by using the arms, the offender shall be punished with imprisonment for life.

The offence as provided in the first paragraph, if the offender being the man commits against the girl over thirteen years but not yet over fifteen years of age with her consent and the Court grants such man and girl to marry together afterwards, the offender shall not be punished for such offence. If the Court grants them to marry together during the offender be still inflicted with the punishment, the Court shall release such offender.

Section 277 bis If the commission of the offence according to the first paragraph of Section 276, or the first or second paragraph of Section 277, causes:

1. Grievous bodily harm to the victim, the offender shall be punished with imprisonment of fifteen to twenty

years and fined of thirty thousand to forty thousand Baht, or imprisonment for life;

2. Death to the victim, the offender shall be punished with death or imprisonment for life.

Section 277 ter If the commission of the offence according to the second paragraph of Section 276 or the third paragraph of Section 277, causes: Grievous bodily harm to the victim, the offender shall be punished with death or imprisonment for life Death to the victim, the offender shall be punished with death.

Section 278 Whoever, committing an indecent act to the person out of fifteen years of age by threatening with any means, by doing any act of violence, by taking advantage of that person to be in the condition of inability to resist, or by causing that person to mistake him for the other person, shall be imprisoned not out of ten years or fined not out of twenty thousand Baht, or both.

Section 279 Whoever, commits an indecent act on a child not yet over fifteen years of age, whether such child shall consent or not, shall be punished with imprisonment not exceeding ten years or fined not exceeding twenty thousand Baht, or both.

If the commission of the offence according to the first paragraph, the offender commits it by threatening by any means whatever, by doing any act of violence, by taking advantage of such child being in the condition of inability to resist, or by causing such child to mistake him for another person, the offender shall be punished with imprisonment not exceeding fifteen years or fined not exceeding thirty thousand Baht, or both.

Section 280 If the commission of offence according to the Section 278 or Section 279 causes:

1. Grievous bodily harm to the victim, the offender shall be punished with imprisonment of five to twenty years and fined of ten thousand to forty thousand Baht;

2. Death to the victim, the offender shall be punished with death or imprisonment for life.

Section 281 The commission of offence according to the paragraph 1 of Section 276 and Section 278, if not to occur in the public, not to cause the grievous bodily harm or death to the victim, not commit against the person as specified in this Section, it shall be the compoundable offence.

Section 282 Whoever, in order to gratify the sexual desire of another person, procures, seduces or takes away for indecent act the man or woman with his or her consent, shall be punished with imprisonment of one to ten years and fined of two thousand to twenty thousand Baht.

If the commission of the offence according to the first paragraph is occurred to the person over fifteen years but not yet over eighteen years of age, the offender shall be punished with imprisonment of three to fifteen years and fined of six thousand to thirty thousand Baht.

If the commission of the offence according to the first paragraph is occurred to the child not yet over fifteen years of age, the offender shall be punished with imprisonment of five to twenty years and fined of ten thousand to forty thousand Baht. Whoever, in order to gratify the sexual desire of another person, obtains the person who is procured, seduced or taken away according to the first, second or third paragraph or supports in such commission of offence, shall be liable to the punishment as provided in the first, second or third paragraph, as the case may be.

Section 283 Whoever, in order to gratify the sexual desire of another person, procures, seduces or takes away for indecent act a man or woman by using deceitful means, threat, doing an act of violence, unjust influence or mode of coercion by any other means, shall be punished with imprisonment of five to twenty years and fined of ten thousand to forty thousand Baht.

If the commission of the offence according to the first paragraph is occurred to the person over fifteen years but not yet over eighteen years of age, the offender shall be punished with imprisonment of seven to twenty years and fined of fourteen thousand to forty thousand Baht, or imprisonment for life.

If the commission of the offence according to the first paragraph is occurred to the child not yet over fifteen years of age, the offender shall be punished with imprisonment of ten to twenty years and fined twenty thousand to forty thousand Baht, or imprisonment for life, or death.

Whoever, in order to gratify the sexual desire of another person, obtains the person who is procured, seduced or taken away according to the first, second or third paragraph, or supports in such commission of offence, shall be liable to the punishment as provided in the first, second or third paragraph, as the case may be.

Section 283 bis Whoever, takes away the person over fifteen years but not yet over eighteen years of age for indecent act with consent of such person, shall be punished with imprisonment of not exceeding five years or fined not exceeding ten thousand Baht, or both.

If the commission of offence according to the first paragraph is occurred to the child not yet over the fifteen years of age, the offender shall be punished with imprisonment not exceeding seven years or fined not exceeding fourteen thousand Baht, or both.

Whoever conceals the person, who is taken away according to the first or second paragraph, shall be liable to punishment as provided in the first or second paragraph, as the case may be.

If the offences according to the first and third paragraph are specially occurred in the case of committing to the person exceeding the fifteen years of age, they are compoundable offences.

Section 284 Whoever, takes away an another person for indecent act by using deceitful means, threat, doing any act of violence, unjust influence or mode of coercion by any other means, shall be punished with imprisonment of one of ten years and fined of two thousand to twenty thousand Baht.

Whoever conceals the person, who is taken away according to the first paragraph, shall be liable to the same punishment as the person who takes away.

The offence according to this Section is compoundable offence.

Section 285 If committing the offence under Section 276, Section 277 bis, Section 277 ter, Section 278, Section 279, Section 280, Section 282 or Section 283 to be act against the descendant, pupil under taken one self's care, person under one self's control according to oneself official authority, or person under one self's tutorship, guardianship or courtship, such offender shall be punished by the heavier punishment then that as prescribed in that Section by one-third.

Section 286 Any person, being over sixteen years of age, subsists on the earning of a prostitute, even it is some part of her incomes, shall be punished with imprisonment of seven to twenty years and fined of fourteen thousand to forty thousand Baht, or imprisonment for life.

Any person has no other apparent or sufficient means of subsistence, and:

1. Is found residing or habitually associating with one or more prostitutes;

2. Takes board and lodging, or receives money or any other benefit arranged for by a prostitute; or

3. Take part in order to help any prostitute in her quarrel with her customer,

The provisions of this Section shall not be applied to any person who receives maintenance from a prostitute who is bound to give maintenance according to law or morality.

Section 287 Whoever:

1. For the purpose of trade or by trade, for public distribution or exhibition, makes, produces, possesses, brings or causes to be brought into the Kingdom, sends or causes to be sent out of the Kingdom, takes away or causes to be taken away, or circulates by any means

whatever, any document, drawing, print, painting, printed matter, picture, poster, symbol, photograph, cinematograph film, noise tape, picture tape or any other thing which is obscene;

2. Carries on trade, or takes part or participates in the trade concerning the aforesaid obscene material or thing, or distributes or exhibits to the public, or hires out such material or thing;

3. In order to assist in the circulation or trading of the aforesaid obscene material or thing, propagates or spreads the news by any means whatever that there is a person committing the act which is an offence according to this Section, or propagates or spreads the news that the aforesaid obscene material or thing may be obtained from any person or by any means, shall be punished with imprisonment not exceeding three years or fined not exceeding six thousand Baht, or both.

CHAPTER 2

OFFENCE CAUSING DEATH

Section 288 Whoever, murdering the other person, shall be imprisoned by death or imprisoned as from fifteen years to twenty years.

Section 289 Whoever commits murder on:
1. An ascendant;

2. An official in the exercise of his functions, or by reason of exercising or having exercised his functions;

3. A person who assists an official in the exercise of his functions, or by reason of the fact that such person will assist or has assisted the said official;

4. The other person by premeditation;

5. The other person by employing torture or acts of cruelty;

6. The other person for the purpose of preparing or facilitating the commission of the other offence; or

7. The other person for the purpose of securing the benefit obtained through the other offence, or concealing the

other offence or escaping punishment for the other offence committed by him, shall be punished with death.

Section 290 Whoever, causes death to the other person by inflicting injury upon the body of such person without intent to cause death, shall be punished with imprisonment of three to fifteen years.

If the offence being committed under any of the circumstances mentioned in Section 289, the offender shall be punished with imprisonment of three to twenty years.

Section 291 Whoever, doing the act by negligence and that act causing the other person to death, shall be imprisoned not out of ten years or fined not out of twenty thousand Baht.

Section 292 Whoever, practicing the cruelty or employing the similar factor on the person to have depended on him for subsistence or any other activities so as to that person shall commit the suicide, if suicide to have occurred or to have been attempted, shall be imprisoned not out seven years and fined not out of fourteen thousand Baht.

Section 293 Whoever aids or instigates a child not over sixteen years of age, or a person who is unable to understand the nature and importance of his act or who is unable to control his act, to commit suicide, shall, if suicide has occurred or has been attempted, be punished with imprisonment not exceeding five years or fined not exceeding ten thousand Baht, or both.

Section 294 Whoever, in as affray among three persons upwards, and any person, whether such person to be participant in such affray or not, to be death, shall be imprisoned not out of two years or fined not out of four thousand Baht, or both.
If the participant in such affray can show that oneself has acted so as to prevent such affray or to prevent lawfully, such participant shall not be punished.

CHAPTER 3

OFFENCE AGAINST BODY

Section 295 Whoever, causes injury to the other person in body or mind is said to commit bodily harm, and shall be punished with imprisonment not exceeding two years or fined not exceeding four thousand Baht, or both.

Section 296 Whoever, committing bodily harm, if such offence having any circumstance as prescribed by Section 289, shall be imprisoned not out of three years or fined not out of six thousand Baht, or both.

Section 297 Whoever, commits bodily harm, and thereby causing the victim to receive grievous bodily harm, shall be punished with imprisonment of six months to ten years. Grievous bodily harms are as follows:

1. Deprivation of the sight, deprivation of the hearing, cutting of the tongue or loss of the sense of smelling;
2. Loss of genital organs or reproductive ability;

3. Loss of an arm, leg, hand, foot, finger or any other organ;

4. Permanent disfiguration of face;

5. Abortion;

6. Permanent insanity;

7. Infirmity or chronic illness which may last throughout life;

Infirmity or illness causing the sufferer to be in severe bodily pain for over twenty days or to be unable to follow the ordinary pursuits for over twenty days.

Section 298 Whoever, committing the offence under Section 297 under any circumstance as prescribed by Section 289, shall be imprisoned as from two years to ten years.

Section 299 Whenever, grievous bodily harm is caused to any person in an affray in which three persons upwards are engaged, whether such person be a participant in such affray or not, the participants in such affray shall be punished with imprisonment not exceeding one year or fined not exceeding two thousand Baht, or both.

If the participant in such affray can show that he has acted in order to prevent such affray or in lawful defense, he shall not be punished.

Section 300 Whoever, committing the act by negligence and such act to cause the grievous bodily harm to the other person, shall be imprisoned three years or fined not out of six thousand Baht, or both.

CHAPTER 4

OFFENCE OF ABORTION

Section 301 Any woman, causing herself to be aborted or allowing the other person to procure the abortion for herself, shall be imprisoned not out of three years or fined not out of six thousand Baht, or both.

Section 302 Whoever, procures abortion for a woman with her consent, shall be punished with imprisonment not exceeding five years or fined not exceeding ten thousand Baht, or both. If such act causes other grievous bodily harm to the woman also, the offender shall be punished with imprisonment not exceeding seven years or fined not exceeding fourteen thousand Baht, or both. If such act causes death to the woman, the offender shall be punished with imprisonment not exceeding ten years and fined not exceeding twenty thousand Baht.

Section 303 Whoever, procures abortion for a woman without her consent, shall be punished with imprisonment not exceeding seven years or fined not exceeding fourteen thousand Baht, or both. If such act causes other grievous bodily harm to the woman also, the offender shall be punished with imprisonment of one to ten years and fined of two thousand to twenty thousand Baht.

If such act causes death to the woman, the offender shall be punished with imprisonment of five to twenty years and fined of ten thousand to forty thousand Baht.

Section 304 Whoever, attempts to commit the offence according to Section 301 or Section 302, first paragraph, shall not be punished.

Section 305 If the offence mentioned in Section 301 and Section 302, be committed by a medical practitioner, and:

1. It is necessary for the sake of the health of such woman; or

2. The woman is pregnant on account of the commission of the offence as provided in Section 276, Section 277, Section 282, Section 283 or Section 284 the offenders not guilty.

3.

CHAPTER 5

OFFENCE OF ABANDONMENT OF CHILDREN, SICK PERSONS OR AGED PERSONS

Section 306 Whoever, abandons a child not over nine years of age in any place, with intent to wholly abandon such child in a manner so that such child shall be without a person to take care of, shall be punished with imprisonment not exceeding three years or fined not exceeding six thousand Baht, or both.

Section 307 Whoever, to have the duty according to the law or the have the contract taking care of the person in the helpless condition through age, because of sickness, infirmity in body or mind, abandoning such person in the manner likely to endanger his or her life, shall be imprisoned out of three years or fined not out of six thousand Baht, or both.

Section 308 If the commission of the offence according to Section 306 or Section 307 causes death or grievous bodily harm to the abandoned person, the offender shall be punished as provided in Section 290, Section 297 or Section 298.

CHAPTER 6

OFFENCE AGAINST LIBERTY

Section 309 Whoever, compels the other person to do or not to do any act, or to suffer any thing by putting him in fear of injury to life, body, liberty, reputation or property of him or another person, or commits violence so that he does or does not do such a ct, or suffers such thing, shall be punished with imprisonment not exceeding three years or fined not exceeding six thousand Baht, or both. If the offence according to the first paragraph be committed by ma king use of arms or by five persons upwards participating, or it be committed in order that the compelled person shall execute, revoke, damage or destroy any document of right, the offender shall be punished with imprisonment not exceeding five years or fined not exceeding ten thousand Baht, or both.

If the offence be committed by alluding to the p ower of the secret society or criminal association, whether it be existent or not, the offender shall be punished with imprisonment of one to seven years and fined of two thousand to fourteen thousand Baht.

Section 310 Whoever, detains or confines the other person, or by any other means whatever, deprives
such person of the liberty of person, shall be punished with imprisonment not exceeding three years or fined not exceeding six thousand Baht, or both. If the commission of the offence according to the first paragraph causes death or grievous bodily harm to the person detained, confined or deprived of the liberty of person, the offender shall be punished as provided in Section 290, Section 297 or Section 298.

Section 310 bis Whoever, detaining or confining the other person or making in any manner to deprive other person without liberty bodily and making such other person to do any act for the doer or other person, shall be imprisoned not out of five years or fined not out of ten thousand Baht.

Section 311 Whoever, by negligence causes the other person to be detained, confined or deprived of the liberty of person, shall be punished with imprisonment not exceeding one year or fined not exceeding two thousand Baht, or both. If the commission of the offence according to the first paragraph causes death or grievous bodily harm to the person detained, confined or deprived of the liberty of person, the offender shall be punished as provided in Section 291 or 300.

Section 312 Whoever, so as to enslave the person or to cause the person t o be in the position similar to the slave, bringing into or sending out of the Kingdom, removing, buying, selling, disposing, accepting or restraining any person, shall be impr isoned not out of seven years and fined not out of fourteen thousand Baht.

Section 312 bis If the commission of the offence according to Section 310 bis or Section 312 is committed to the child not exceeding fifteen years of age, the offender shall be punish ed with imprisonment of three to ten years and fined not exceeding twenty thousand Baht. If the commission of the offence according to the first paragraph or Section 310 bis or Section 312 causes:

1. Bodily harm or mental harm to the victim, the offender shall be punished with imprisonment of five to fifteen years and fined not exceeding thirty thousand Baht;

2. Grievous bodily harm to the victim, the offender shall be punished with imprisonment for life or imprisonment of seven to twenty years;

3. Death to the victim, the offender shall be punished with death, imprisonment for life or imprisonment of fifteen to twenty years.

Section 312 ter Whoever, by dishonestly, a accepting, disposing, procuring, seducing or taking away the person over fifteen years but not yet over eighteen years of age by such person's consent, shall be imprisoned not out of five years or fined not out of ten thousand Baht, or both. If the committing the offence according to paragraph 1 committed to the child not yet out of fifteen years of age, such offender shall be not out of seven years or fined not out of fourteen thousand Baht, or both.

Section 313 Whoever, in order to obtain a ransom:

1. Takes away a child not yet over fifteen years of age;

2. Takes away a person over fifteen years of age by using deceitful means, threat, doing any act of violence, unjust influence or mode of coercion by any other means; or

3. Restrains or detains any person, shall be punished with imprisonment of fifteen to twenty years and fined of thirty thousand to forty thousand Baht, or imprisonment for life, or death.

If the commission of the offence according to the first paragraph causes grievous bodily harm to such person taken away, restrained or detained, or is by acts of torture or hardly cruelty so as to cause bodily harm or mental harm to such person, the offender shall be punished with death or imprisonment for life. If the commission of such offence causes death to the person taken away, restrained or detained, the offender shall be punished with death.

Section 314 Whoever, to be a supporter to the commission of the offence according to Section 313, shall be liable to the same punishment as a principal in such offence.

Section 315 Whoever, to act as the intermediary person, to demanding, accepting or agreeing to acceptant property or benefit to which not to be entitled from the offender under Section 313 or from the person who will give the ransom, shall be imprisoned as from fifteen years to twenty years and fined as from thirty thousand Baht to forty thousand Baht, or li fe imprisonment.

Section 316 If the offender a cording to Section 313, Section 314 or Section 315 arranges for the person who is taken away, restrained or confined to regain his liberty before the judgment of the Court of First Instance without receiving grievous bodily harm or being in the condition of imminent danger to life, such offender shall be in flicted with less punishment than that provided by the law, but not less than one-half.

Section 317

Whoever, without reasonable cause, takes away a child not yet over fifteen years of age from the parent, guardian or person looking after such child, shall be punished with imprisonment of three to fifteen years and fined of six thousand to thirty thousand Baht.

Whoever dishonestly buys, disposes of or accepts such child to taken away according to the first paragraph, shall be liable to the same punishment as the person who takes the child away. If the offence of this Section has committed for lucre or indecent purpose, the offender shall be punished with imprisonment of five to twenty years and fined of ten thousand to forty thousand Baht.

Section 318 Whoever, takes away a minor over fifteen yea rs but not yet over eighteen years of age from the parent, guardian or person looking after such minor against a will of such minor, shall be punished with imprisonment of tw o to ten years and fined of four thousand to tw enty thousand Baht.

Whoever dishonestly buys, disposes of or accepts a minor to taken away according to the first paragraph, shall be liable to the same punishment as the person who takes such minor away.

If the offence according to this Section has committed for lucre or indecent purpose, the offender shall be punished with imprisonment of three to fifteen years and fined of six thousand to thirty thousand Baht.

Section 319 Whoever, takes away a minor over fifteen years of age but not yet over eighteen years of
age from the parent, guardian or person looking after such minor for lucre or indecent purpose with the consent of such minor, shall be punished with imprisonment of two to ten years and fined of four thousand to twenty thousand Baht. Whoever dishonestly buys, disposes, or accepts a minor to taken away according to the first paragraph, shall be liable to the same punishment as the person who takes such minor away.

Section 320 Whoever, by using fraudulent or deceitful means, threat, violence, unjust influence or another means of compulsion, takes or sends a person out of the Kingdom, shall be punished with imprisonment of two to ten years or fined of four thousand to twenty thousand Baht, or both. If the commission of the offence according to the first pa rewrap be committed in order that the person taken or sent out to be under the power of the other person unlawfully, or in order to abandon such person to be in a helpless condition, the offender shall be punished with imprisonment of three to fifteen years and fined of six thousand to thirty thousand Baht.

Section 321 The offence under Section 309, the first paragraph, Section 310, the first paragraph, and Section 311, the first paragraph, are the compoundable offences.

CHAPTER 7

OFFENCE OF DISCLOSURE OF PRIVATE SECRETS

Section322 Whoever, breaking open or taking away the closed letter, telegram or any document belonging to the other person so as to ascertain or to disclose its contents, if such act to be likely to cause injury to any person, shall be imprisoned not out of six months or fined not out of one thousand Baht, or both.

Section 323 Whoever, knows or acquires a private secret of another person by reason of his functions asa competent official or his profession as a medical practitioner, pharmacist, druggist, midwife, nursing attendant, priest, advocate, lawyer or auditor, or by reason of being an assistant in such profession, and then discloses such private secret in a manner likely to cause injury to any person, shall be punished with imprisonment not exceeding six months or fined not exceeding one thousand Baht, or both.

A person undergoing training and instruction in the profession mentioned in the first paragraph has known or acquired the private secret of another person in the training and instruction in such profession, and discloses such private secret in a manner likely to cause injury to any person, shall be liable to the same punishment.

Section 324 Whoever, on the ground that oneself having the duty, professing to call the trust, having known or acquired the secret according to industry, discovery or scientific invention, disclosing or using such secret for the benefit of oneself or other person, shall be imprisoned not out of six months or fined not out of one thousand Baht, or both.

Section 325 The offences in this Chapter are compoundable offences.

CHAPTER 8

OFFENCE OF DEFAMATION

Section 326 Whoever, imputes anything to the other person before a third person in a manner likely to impair the reputation of such other person or to expose such other person to be hated or scorned, is said to commit defamation, and shall be punished with imprisonment not exceeding one year or fined not exceeding twenty thousand Baht, or both.

Section 327 Whoever, imputing anything the deceased person before the third person, and that imputation to be likely to impair the reputation of the father, mother, spouse or child of the deceased or to expose that person hated or scammed to be said to commit defamation, and shall be punished as prescribed by Section 326.

Section 328 If the offence of defamation be committed by means of publication of a document, drawing, painting, cinematography film, picture or letters made visible by any means, gramophone record or another recording instruments, recording picture or letters, or by broadcasting or spreading picture, or by propagation by any other means, the offender shall be punished with imprisonment not exceeding two years and fined not exceeding two hundred thousand Baht.

Section 329 Whoever, in good faith, expresses any opinion or statement:

1. By way of self justification or defense, or for the protection of a legitimate interest;

2. In the status of being an official in the exercise of his functions;

3. By way of fair comment on any person or thing subjected to public criticism; or

4. By way of fair report of the open proceeding of any Court or meeting, shall not be guilty of defamation.

Section 330 In case of defamation, if the person prosecuted for defamation can prove that the imputation made by him is true, he shall not be punished. But he shall not be allowed to prove if such imputation concerns personal matters, and such proof will not be benefit to the public.

Section 331 The party in a case or party's lawyer expressing opinion or statement in the proceeding of the Court in favor of his case shall not be offence of defamation.

Section 332 In case of defamation in which judgment is given that the accused is guilty, the Court may give order:

1. To seize and destroy the defamatory matter or part thereof;

2. To publish the whole or part of the judgment in one or more newspapers once or several times at the expense of the accused.

Section 333 The offences in this Chapter are compoundable offences. If the injured person in the defamation dies before making a complaint, the father, mother, spouse or child of the deceased may make a complaint, and it shall be deemed that such person is the injured person.

CHAPTER 10

OFFENCE OF THEFT AND SNATCHING

Section 334 Whoever, dishonestly taking away the thing of other person or which the other person to bacon-owner to be said to commit the theft, shall be imprisoned not out of three years and fined not out of six thousand Baht.

Section 335 Whoever commits theft under any of the following circumstances:

1. By night;

2. In the place or precinct where there is fire, explosion, flood, or in the place or precinct where there is an accident, distress to railway or other public

conveyance

or other similar calamity, or by taking advantage of such accident, distress or calamity, or by taking advantage of any public panic;

3. By damaging a barricade made for the protection of persons or things, or by penetrating through such barricade by any means whatever;

4. By using a passage not intended for human entrance, or a passage opened by an accomplice;

5. By disguising himself, or by impersonating another person, or by blackening his face or doing otherwise so that he may not be seen or recognized;

6. By falsely pretending that he is an official;

7. By carrying arms, or by having two persons upwards participating;

8. In a dwelling place, official place or place provided for public service which he has entered without permission, or has hidden himself therein;

9. In a place of public worship, a railway station, an airport, a public parking or mooring place for cars or boats, a public place for loading and discharging

goods or in a public conveyance ;

10. Upon a thing used or possessed for public benefit;

11. Upon a thing belonging to or in possession of the employer;

12. Upon a thing belonging to an agriculturist, which is a product, plant, animal or implement possessed for the purpose of carrying on agricultural pursuit or acquired from such agricultural pursuit,

Shall be punished with imprisonment of one to five years and fined of two thousand to ten thousand Baht.

If the offence committed according to the first paragraph comes under the circumstances provided in the above-mentioned sub-sections from two sub-sections upwards also, the offender shall be punished with imprisonment of one to seven years and fined of two thousand to fourteen thousand Baht.

If the offence according to the first paragraph be committed against the ox, buffalo, mechanical device or machinery of the agriculturist to possess for purpose of carrying on agricultural pursuit, the offender shall be punished with imprisonment of three to ten years and fined of six thousand to twenty thousand Baht.

If the offence mentioned in this Section be committed against the will or on account of unbearable poverty, and the property stolen is of little value, the Court may inflict the punishment on the offender as provided in Section 334.

Section 335 bis Whoever, commits theft by taking away the Buddhist Statue, religious object, or any part thereof, which is possessed for the public to worship or kept for being the property of Nation, shall be punished with imprisonment of three to ten years and fined of six thousandth twenty thousand Baht.

If the commission of offence according to the first paragraph be committed in the temple, dwelling place of the monks, religious worship place, ancient place of the State, official place or National museum, the offender shall be punished with imprisonment of five to fifteen years and fined of ten thousand to thirty thousand Baht.

Section 336 Whoever, commits theft by snatching in presence is said to commit snatching, and shall be punished with imprisonment not exceeding five years and fined not exceeding ten thousand Baht. If the snatching causes bodily or mental harm to another person, the offender shall be punished with imprisonment of two to seven years and fined of four thousand to fourteen thousand Baht. If the snatching causes grievous
bodily harm to another person, the offender shall be punished with imprisonment of three to ten years and fined of six thousand to twenty thousand Baht.

If the snatching causes death to another person, the offender shall be punished with imprisonment of five to fifteen years and fined of ten thousand to thirty thousand Baht.

Section 336 bis

Whoever, committing the offence under Section 334, Section 335, Section 335 bis, or

Section 336 by wearing the soldier or police uniform or dressing so as to cause the other person to believe that oneself to be the soldier or police, or by carrying or using the gun or explosive, or using the conveyance so as to facilitate in committing the offence, to takeaway such thing or escape from the arrest, shall be punished more than that as prescribed in such Section by half.

CHAPTER 11

OFFENCE OF EXTORTION, BLACKMAIL, ROBBERY AND GANG-ROBBERY

Section 337 Whoever, compels a person to give or to agree to give him or the other person a benefit in the nature of being a property by committing an act of violence or by a threat to commit violence against the life, body, liberty, reputation or property of the compelled person or a third person, so that the compelled person submits to the same is said to commit extortion, and shall be punished with imprisonment not exceeding five years and fined not exceeding ten thousand Baht. If extortion be committed:

1. By threat ending to cause death or grievous bodily harm to the compelled person or the other person or to set fire to the property of the compelled person or other person; or

2. By a person carrying an arm, the offender shall be punished with imprisonment of six months to seven years and fined of one thousand to fourteen thousand Baht.

Section 338

Whoever, compelling the other person to give or to agree to give oneself or the other person the benefit in the nature to be the property by threatening to disclose the secret, to cause injury to the compelled person or the third person, up to the compelled person submit to the same, such person to be said to commit blackmail, and shall be imprisoned as from one year to ten years and fined as from two thousand Baht to twenty thousand Baht.

Section 339

Whoever, commits theft by doing any act of violence or threatening to do any act of violence immediately in order:

1. To facilitate the theft or taking away of the thing;

2. To obtain delivery of the thing;

3. To take hole of the thing;

4. To conceal the commission of such offence; or

5. To escape from arrest, is said to commit robbery , and shall be punished with imprisonment of five

to ten years and fined of ten thousand to twenty thousand Baht.

If such offence is committed under the circumstances as provided in any subsection of Section 335, or being to commit against the ox, buffalo, mechanical device or machinery of the agriculturist to possess for purpose of carrying on agricultural pursuit, the offender shall be punished with imprisonment of ten to fifteen years and fined of twenty thousand to thirty thousand Baht.

If the robbery causes bodily or mental harm to the other person, the offender shall be punished with imprisonment of ten to twenty years and fined of twenty thousand to forty thousand Baht.

If the robbery causes grievous bodily harm to the other person, the offender shall be punished with imprisonment of fifteen to twenty years and fined of thirty thousand to forty thousand Baht. If the robbery causes death to the other person, the offender shall be punished with death or imprisonment for life.

Section 339 bis If the robbery is committed against the thing according to the first paragraph of Section 335bis, the offender shall be punished with imprisonment of ten to fifteen years and fined of twenty thousand to thirty thousand Baht. If such robbery is committed in the place as provided in the second paragraph of Section 335 bis also, the offender shall be punished with imprisonment of ten to twenty years and fined of twenty thousand to forty thousand Baht.

If the robbery according to the first and second paragraph causes bodily or mental harm to the other person, the offender shall be punished with imprisonment of fifteen to twenty years and fined of thirty thousand to forty thousand Baht.

If the robbery according to the first or the second paragraph causes grievous bodily harm to the other person, the offender shall be punished with imprisonment for life or imprisonment of fifteen to twenty years. If the robbery according to the first or second paragraph causes death to the other person, the offender shall be punished with death.

Section 340

Whoever with three persons upwards participate in committing robbery, such persons are said to commit gang-robbery, and shall be punished with imprisonment of ten to fifteen years and fined of twenty thousand to thirty thousand Baht.

If in the commission of the gang-robbery, even one of the offenders carries arms, the offender shall be punished with imprisonment of twelve to twenty years and fined of twenty-four thousand to forty thousand Baht. If the gang-robbery causes grievous bodily harm to the other person, the offender shall be punished with imprisonment for life or imprisonment of fifteen to twenty years.

If the gang-robbery is committed by acts of cruelty so as to cause bodily or mental harm to the other person, by shooting with a gun, by using explosive or by acts of torture, the offender shall be punished with imprisonment for life or imprisonment of fifteen to twenty years. If the gang-robbery causes death to the other person, the offender shall be punished with death.

Section 340 bis If the gang-robbery is committed against the things according to the first paragraph of Section 335 bis, the offender shall be punished with imprisonment of ten to twenty year sand find of twenty thousand to forty thousand Baht.

If such gang-robbery is committed in the place as provided in the second paragraph of Section 335 bis also, the offender shall be punished with imprisonment of fifteen to twenty years and fined of thirty thousand to forty thousand Baht. If the gang-robbery according to the first or second paragraph, even one of the offenders carries arms, the offender shall be punished with imprisonment for life or imprisonment of fifteen to twenty years. If the gang-robbery according to the first or second paragraph causes grievous bodily harm to the other person, the offender shall be punished with imprisonment for life.If the gang-robbery according to the first or second paragraph is committed by acts of cruelty so as to cause bodily or mental harm to the other person, by shooting with a gun, by using explosive or by acts of torture, the offende r shall be punished with death or imprisonment for life.

If the gang-robbery according to the first or second paragraph causes death to the other person, the offender shall be punished with death.

Section 340 ter
Whoever, committing the offence under Section 339, Section 339 bis, Section 340 or Section 340 bis, by wearing the soldier or police uniform, by dressing so as to mistake for the soldier or police, or by carrying or using the gun or explosive, or by using the conveyance so as to commit the offence for taking such thing away or for escaping from the arrest, shall be punished to heavier punishment than that as prescribed by such Section by half.

CHAPTER 12

OFFENCE OF CHEATING AND FRAUD

Section 341

Whoever, dishonestly deceives a person with the assertion of a falsehood or the concealment of the facts which should be revealed, and, by such deception, obtains a property from the person so deceived or a third person, or causes the person so deceived oar third person to execute, revoke or destroy a document of right, is said to commit the offence of cheating and fraud, and shall be punished with imprisonment not exceeding three years or fined not exceeding six thousand Baht, or both.

Section 342 If the offence of cheating and fraud be committed:

1. By the offender showing himself to be another person; found on www.samuiforsale.com or

2. By taking advantage of the lack of intelligence of the deceived person who is a child, or by ta king advantage of weakness of mind of the deceived person,

The offender shall be punished with imprisonment not exceeding five years or fined not exceeding ten thousand Baht, or both.

Section 343 If the offence under Section 341 be committed by the assertion of a falsehood to the public or by the concealment of the fa cts which should be revealed to the public, the offender shall be punished with imprisonment not exceeding five years or fined not exceeding ten thousand Baht, or both.

If the offence mentioned in the first paragraph b e committed under the circumstances mentioned in any sub-section of Section 342 also, the offender shall be punished with imprisonment of six months to seven years and fined of one thousand to fourteen thousand Baht.

Section 344 Whoever, dishonestly, deceiving ten persons upwards to perform any work for oneself or for the third person with the intent not to pay the wages or remuneration to such persons, or with the intent to pay such persons lower wages or remuneration than those agreed upon, shall be imprisoned not out of three years or fined not out of six thousand Baht, or both.

Section 345

Whoever, orders and consumes food or drink, or stays in a hotel, by knowing that the he cannot pay money for the food, drink or the stay in the hotel, shall be punished with imprisonment not exceeding three months or fined not exceeding five hundred Baht, or both.

Section 346

Whoever, in order to take a property of another person for himself or a third person, induces any person to dispose of the property at a disadvantage on account of the induced person being weak-minded, or being a child lacking in intelligence and being unable to understand reasonably the essentials of his acts so that the induced person submits to the disposal of such property, shall be punished with imprisonment not exceeding two years or fined not exceeding four thousand Baht, or both.

Section 347

Whoever, so as to oneself or the other person to

obtain the benefit the insurance, maliciously causing the danger to the insured property, shall be imprisoned not out of five years or fined not out of two thousand Baht, or both.

Section 348

The offences in this Chapter excepting the offence under Section 343 are compoundable offences.

CHAPTER 13

OFFENCE OF CHEATING AGAINST CREDITORS

Section 349

Whoever, taking away, damaging, destroying, causing depreciation of value, or rendering useless the property to have been pledged to another person, if being commission so as to cause injury to the pledged, shall be imprisoned not out of two years or fined not out of four thousand Baht, or both.

Section 350 Whoever, in order to prevent his creditor or the creditor of the other person from receiving payment in whole or in part which has been or will be claimed through the Court, removes, conceals or transfers any property to another person, or maliciously contracts a debt for any sum which is not true, shall be punished with imprisonment not exceeding two years or fined not exceeding four thousand Baht, or both. Section 351The offences in this Chapter are compoundable offences.

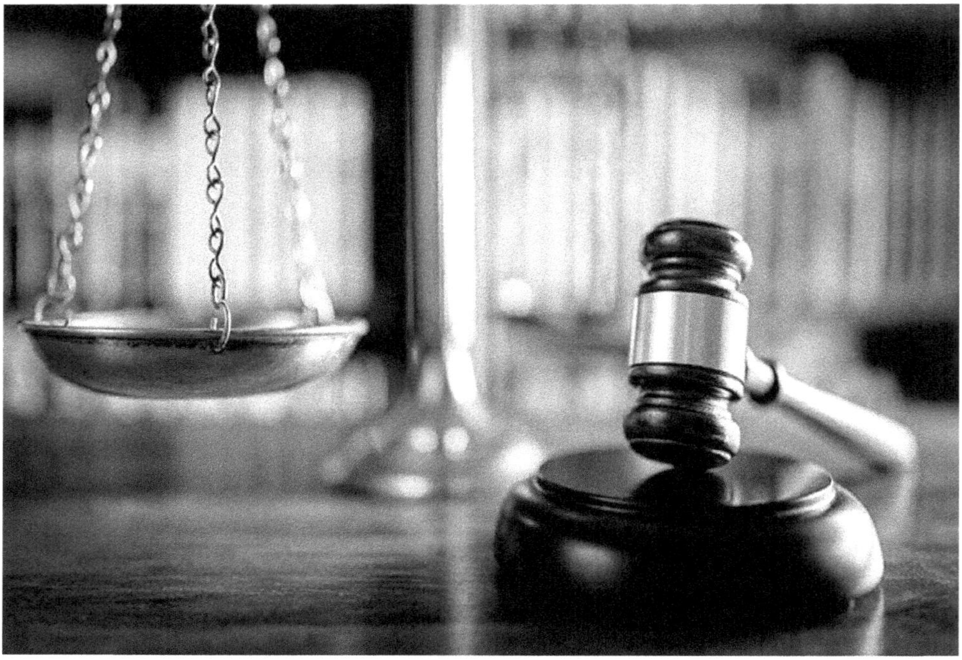

CHAPTER 14

OFFENCE OF MISAPPROPRIATION

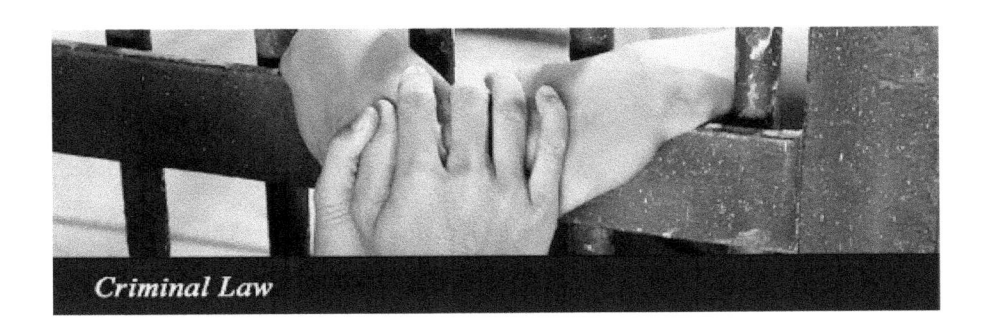

Section 352 Whoever, being in possession of a property belonging to the other person, or of which the other person is a co-owner, dishonestly convert s such property to himself or a third person, is said to commit misappropriation, and shall be punished with imprisonment not exceeding three years or fined not exceeding six thousand Baht, or both. If such property comes under the possession of the offender on account of being delivered to him by the other person by mistake by any means whatever, or being a l ost property found by him, the offender shall be liable to one-half of the punishment.

Section **353**

Whoever, to be entrusted to manage the other person's property or property which the other person to be the co-owner, dishonestly to do any act contrary to oneself duty by any means whatever, up to cause the danger to the benefit on account of being the property of such other person, shall be imprisoned not out of three years or fined not out of six thousand Baht, or both. Section 354If the offence under Section 352 or Section 353 be committed by the offender in the status of being an executor or administrator of the property of the other person under the order of the Court or under a will, or in the status of being a person having an occupation or business of public trust, the offender shall be punished with imprisonment not exceeding five years or fined not exceeding ten thousand Baht, or both.

Section 355 Whoever, to have found the valuable movable property to be hidden or buried under the circumstances of which no person claim to be the owner, to have converted such property for oneself or the other person, shall be imprisoned not out of one year or fined not out of two thousand Baht, or both.

Section 356 The offences in this Chapter are compoundable offences.

CHAPTER 15

OFFENCE OF RECEIVING STOLEN PROPERTY

Section   **357**

Whoever, assists in concealing, disposing of, making away with, purchases, receives in pledge or otherwise any property obtained through the commission of an offence, and such offence being theft, snatching, extortion, blackmail, robbery, gang-robbery, cheating and fraud, misappropriation or misappropriation by an official, is said to receive stolen property, and shall be punished with imprisonment not exceeding five years or fined not exceeding ten thousand Baht, or both. If the offence of receiving stolen property be committed for profit or against the property obtained by theft under Section 335 (10), robbery or gang-robbery, the offender shall be punished with imprisonment of six months to ten years and fined of one thousand to twenty thousand Baht. If such offence of receiving stolen property is committed against the property obtained by theft according to Section 335 bis, by the robbery according to Section 339 bis, or by the gang-robbery according to Section 340 bis, the offender shall be punished with imprisonment of five to fifteen years and fined of ten thousand to thirty thousand Baht.

CHAPTER 16

OFFENCE OF MISCHIEF

Section 358 Whoever, damaging, destroying, causing the depreciation of value or rendering useless the property belonging to the other person or which the other person to be the co-owner, such person to be said to commit mischief, and shall be imprisoned not out of three years or fined not out of six thousand Baht, or both.

Section 359 If the offence under Section 358 be committed against:

1. An engine or machinery used for agricultural or industrial pursuits;

2. A cattle;

3. A conveyance or a beast of burden used for public transportation or for agricultural or industrial pursuits; or

4. A plant or produce of an agriculturist, the offender shall be punished with imprisonment not exceeding five years or fined not exceeding ten thousand Baht, or both.

Section 360 Whoever, damaging, destroying, causing the depreciation of value or rendering useless the property used or possessed for public benefit, shall be imprisoned not out of five yours or fined not out of ten thousand Baht, or both.

Section 360 bis Whoever, damages, destroys, causes depreciation in value or renders useless the properties according
to the first paragraph of Section 335 bis, which are stranded in the places according to the second paragraph of Section 335 bis, shall be punished with imprisonment not exceeding ten years or fined not exceeding twenty thousand Baht, or both.

Section 361 The offences under Sections 358 and 359 are compoundable offences.

CHAPTER 17

OFFENCE OF TRESPASS

Section 362 Whoever, entering into the immovable property belonging to the other person so as to take possession of such property in whole or in any part or entering into such property to do any act disturbing the peaceful possession of such person, shall be

imprisoned not out of one year or fined not out of two thousand Baht, or both.

Section 363 Whoever, so as to take hold of the immovable property belonging to the other person for oneself or the third person, removing or destroying the boundary mark or such property in whole or in any party, shall be imprisoned not out of three years or fined not out of six thousand Baht, or both.

Section 364 Whoever, without reasonable cause, enters or hides himself in a dwelling place, store-house or office under the possession of the other person, or refuses to leave such place after having been told to do so by the person having the right to forbid him from entering, shall be punished with imprisonment not exceeding one year or fined not exceeding two thousand Baht, or both.

Section 365 If the offence under Section 362, Section 363 or Section 364 be committed:

1. By an act of violence or threat to commit an act of violence;

2. By a person carrying arms or by two persons upwards pa reticulating; or

3. By night, the offender shall be punished with imprisonment not exceeding five years or fined not exceeding ten thousand Baht, or both.

Section 366 The offences in this Chapter, excepting the offence under Section 365, are compoundable offences.

CHAPTER 18

PETTY OFFENCES

Section 367 Whoever, to have been required by the official to give oneself s name or address for the execution of the law, to refuse to give or give the name or address which to be false, shall be punished by fine not out of one hundred Baht.

Section 368 Whoever, being informed of an order of an official given according to the power invested bylaw, refuses to comply with the same without any reasonable cause or excuse, shall be punished with imprisonment not exceeding ten days or fined not exceeding five hundred Baht, or both. If such order is an order authorized by law requiring a person to assist in carrying on the activities in the function of an official, the offender shall be punished with imprisonment not exceeding one month or fined not exceeding one thousand Baht, or both.

Section 369

Whoever, to act by any means causing the notification, poster or document posted up or exhibited by the official in the excise of one self's duty or by one self's order, to be pulled down, or rendered useless, shall be fined not out of five hundred Baht.

Section 370 Whoever, creates a noise, causes a noise or disturbance without a reasonable cause so as to frighten or trouble the public, shall be punished with fined not exceeding one hundred Baht.

Section 371

Whoever, carries arms in a town, village or public way openly or without a reasonable cause, or carries arms in a gathering assembled for worship, entertainment or any other purpose, shall be punished with fined not exceeding one hundred Baht, and the Court, shall have the power to forfeit such arms.

Section 372 Whoever, quarreling in the public way or place, or causing by any other means to disturb in the public way or place, shall be fined not out of five hundred Baht.

Section 373
Whoever, having the duty to control and to take care of an insane person, allows such insane person to wander about alone, shall be punished with fined not exceeding five hundred Baht.

Section 374 Whoever, to see the other person to be in the danger of life, which oneself may help sop without the danger to oneself or the other person, but oneself does not assist, shall be imprisoned not out of one month or fined not out of one thousand Baht, or both.

Section 375
Whoever, obstructing or causing the inconvenience to the public draw in, watercourse or sewer, shall be fined not out of five hundred Baht.

Section 376

Whoever, unnecessarily fires a gun in a town, village or an other place where there is conglomeration of people, shall be punished with imprisonment not exceeding ten days or fined not exceeding five hundred Baht, or both.

Section 377 Whoever, having in his care a ferocious or vicious animal, allows it to wander about alone in a manner likely to cause injury to a person or things, shall be punished with imprisonment not exceeding one month or fined not exceeding one thousand Baht, or both.

Section 378 Whoever, drinking the spirituous liquor or the other intoxicant up to be drunk, and behaving in the riotous manner, or to be unable to control oneself in any public road or place, shall be fined not out of five hundred Baht.

Section 379

Whoever, in the course of a fight, draws or shows up arms, shall be punished with imprisonment not exceeding ten days or fined not exceeding five hundred Baht, or both.

Section 380

Whoever, causing the water in the well, pond or reservoir provided for public using to be filthy, shall be imprisoned not out of one month or fined not out of one thousand Baht, or both.

Section 381 Whoever, cruelly ill-treats or kills an animal with unnecessary sufferings, shall be punished with imprisonment not exceeding one month or fined not exceeding one thousand Baht, or both.

Section 382

Whoever, overworking the animal unreasonably or using it to do the unsuitable work on account of it to be iii, old or young, shall be imprisoned not out of one month or fined not out of one thousand Baht, or both.

Section 383

Whoever, being called by an official to render assistance in case of fire or other public calamity, fails to comply with such call when he is able to do so, shall be punished with imprisonment not exceeding one moth or fined not exceeding one thousand Baht, or both.

Section 384 Whoever, alarms the public by maliciously circulating false reports, shall be punished with imprisonment not exceeding one month or fined not exceeding one thousand Baht, or both.

Section 385 Whoever, without the lawful permission, unnecessarily obstructing the public way by placing or leaving thereon anything or by acting by any means up to it may interfere with the safety or convenience of traffic, shall be fined not out of five hundred Baht.

Section 386 Whoever, digging the hole or groove, or erecting or placing the cumbrous thing along the public way without the lawful permission, or doing so lawfully but neglecting to show the proper signal to prevent the accident, shall be fined not out of five hundred Baht.

Section 387 Whoever, hangs, installs or places any thing in a manner likely to fall or tumble down and cause injury, dirtiness or trouble to a passer-by in a public way, shall be punished with fined not exceeding five hundred Baht.

Section 388

Whoever, doing any shameful act in public by indecently exposing one self's person, or by committing the other indecent act, shall be fined not out of five hundred Baht.

Section 389 Whoever, by any means whatever, causes a hard substance to fall on any place in a manner likely to cause harm, trouble or nuisance to a person or to cause danger a thing, or by any means whatever, causes a filthy thing to dirty or likely to dirty a person or thing, or maliciously causes a filthy thing to be a trouble or nuisance, shall be punished with imprisonment not exceeding one month or fined not exceeding one thousand Baht, or both.

Section 390

Whoever, causing bodily or mental harm to the other person by negligence, shall be imprisoned not out of one month or fined not out of one thousand Baht, or both.

Section 391 Whoever, commits an act of violence not amounting to bodily or mental harm to the other person, shall be punished with imprisonment not exceeding one month or fined not exceeding one thousand Baht, or both.

Section 392 Whoever, puts a person in fear or in fright by threat, shall be punished with imprisonment not exceeding one month or fined not exceeding one thousand Baht, or both.

Section 393 Whoever, insulting the other person in his presence or by publication, shall be imprisoned not out of one month or fined not out of one thousand Baht, or both.

Section 394 Whoever, chases, drives away or allows any animal to enter a garden, field or farm of the other person, which is prepared, sown or covered with crop, or which contains a produce, shall be punished with imprisonment not exceeding one month or fined not exceeding one thousand Baht, or both.

Section 395
Whoever, having in his care any animal, allows it to enter a garden, field or farm of the other person, which
is prepared, sown or covered with crop, or

which contains a produce, shall be punished with fined not exceeding five hundred Baht.

Section 396

Whoever, leaving the carcass able to be bad to smell on or near the public way, shall be fined not out of five hundred Baht.

Section 397 Whoever, in a public place or before the public, does, by any means whatever to annoy or bully the other person, or causes the other person to be ashamed or troubled, shall be punished with imprisonment not exceeding one month or fined not exceeding one thousand Baht, or both.

Section 398 Whoever, doing by any means to torment the child not yet over fifteen years of age, stickperson or aged person being to depend such person in subsistence or anything else, shall be imprisoned not out of one month of fined not out of one thousand Baht, or both.

Lightning Source UK Ltd.
Milton Keynes UK
UKHW021832040621
384966UK00002B/509